Wildflowers
of Texas

iller

Adventure Quick Guides
YOUR WAY TO EASILY IDENTIFY WILDFLOWERS

Adventure Quick Guides

This statewide Quick Guide highlights more than 248 of the showiest and most common wildflowers seen in Texas, as well as a number of significant rare and endangered species. With thousands of miles of highway roadsides sown with native wildflowers, Texas is known for its diversity of wildflowers. But that's only the start. From the coastal prairies and the rolling hills of Central Texas to the grand prairies of North Texas and the shaded forests of East Texas, Texans eagerly await the annual spring bloom, which often stretches into autumn. Wildflowers are as much a part of the Texas identity as cowboys, longhorns, and barbeque. This Quick Guide will help you put a name to the beautiful wildflowers that decorate the state.

GEORGE MILLER

Longtime botanist and nature photographer, George Miller has explored the West for 30 years. He has written 6 guidebooks to Texas and the Southwest including best sellers *A Field to Wildflowers, Trees, and Shrubs of Texas* and *Landscaping with Native Plants of Texas*, and has published in *Texas Highways, Texas Parks and Wildlife,* and *Wildflowers*, the magazine of the Lady Bird Johnson Wildflower Center. He received a master's degree in zoology and botany from University of Texas, Austin. See his photography and nature articles on his web magazine, Travelsdujour.com.

Cover and book design by Lora Westberg
Edited by Brett Ortler

Cover image: Texas Bluebell by George Miller
All images copyrighted
All images by George Miller

10 9 8 7 6 5 4 3 2

Wildflowers of Texas
Copyright © 2018 by George Miller
Published by Adventure Publications
An imprint of AdventureKEEN
310 Garfield Street South
Cambridge, Minnesota 55008
(800) 678-7006
www.adventurepublications.net
All rights reserved
Printed in China
ISBN 978-1-59193-816-3 (pbk.)

KEY

- Wildflowers are sorted into 4 groups by color and organized within groups from smaller to larger blooms.
- Leaf attachment icons are shown next to each wildflower.
- Descriptions include important facts such as cluster shape, number of petals, or center color to help you quickly identify the species. Size information is sometimes included as well.

LEAF ATTACHMENT

Wildflower leaves attach to stems in different ways. The leaf icons next to the flowers show alternate, opposite, whorled, perfoliate, clasping, and basal attachments. Some wildflower plants have two or more types of leaf attachments.

 ALTERNATE leaves attach in an alternating pattern.

 OPPOSITE leaves attach directly opposite each other.

 BASAL leaves originate at the base of the plant and are usually grouped in pairs or in a rosette.

 PERFOLIATE leaves are stalkless and have a leaf base that completely surrounds the main stem.

 CLASPING leaves have no stalk, and the base partly surrounds the main stem.

 WHORLED leaves have three or more leaves that attach around the stem at the same point.

 CLUSTERED leaves originate from the same point on the stem.

 SPINES are leaves that take the form of sharp spines.

PARTS OF A FLOWER

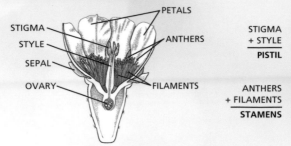

PETALS

STIGMA

STYLE

SEPAL

ANTHERS

OVARY

FILAMENTS

STIGMA
+ STYLE
_____
PISTIL

ANTHERS
+ FILAMENTS
_____
STAMENS

FROM DESERTS TO THE SUBTROPICS

Texas stretches 800 miles from east to west and north to south, and its vast geological, climatic, and biological diversity can bewilder even the most experienced naturalist. The lush Piney Woods of East Texas receive 60 inches of rain annually, while the arid Chihuahuan Desert of El Paso gets a scant 8 inches. The rich blackland prairies around Dallas can have soil 3 feet deep, while the eroded hills of Austin often have more exposed rock than soil. Palm trees line the streets of Brownsville in subtropical South Texas where freezing temperatures are rare, yet thorny mesquite shrubs struggle to survive the droughts and blizzards of Amarillo in the Panhandle, 800 miles north.

Thanks to its climatic and geological diversity, Texas is home to 10 ecological zones, each with its own distinct vegetation. As rainfall and humidity decrease from the Gulf Coast westward to the Trans-Pecos, the vegetation changes from dense forests teeming with plants and wildlife to scrubby junipers and oaks in the savannas of Central Texas. Farther west, prairies and scrubland dominate and trees survive only along waterways. Seven distinct vegetative zones converge in the Big Thicket of East Texas, making it one of the most biologically diverse regions in North America. The isolated mountain ranges of West Texas, with the Guadalupe Mountains exceeding 8,000 feet in elevation, harbor vegetation more common in the Rockies than in the surrounding deserts.

The range of many wildflower species roughly follows these ecological zones, but plants don't respect arbitrary boundaries. Many grow in multiple regions and some occur statewide, while others are limited to just a few Texas counties. This Quick Guide will help you put a name to the beautiful wildflowers that decorate the Lone Star State.

Broomweed

Stems 1–3 feet tall; upper branches form wiry clump; small flower; lance-shaped leaves

Snakeweed

Compact, bushy 1–2-foot stems; flower heads have 3–8 tiny rays; yellow disk; threadlike leaves

Golden Dalea

Stems 1–2 feet tall; flower spike conical, silky with single row of blooms; linear to oval leaflets

Texas Lantana

Shrub 2–6 feet tall; dense cluster has yellow, reddish-orange flowers; sandpapery, triangular leaves

Limoncillo

Low stems to 8 inches tall; flower heads with 8 rays; yellow disk; lemon-scented, linear leaves

Denseflower Bladderpod

Stems 2–12 inches; dense conical flower cluster, 4 petals; spherical fruit; elliptical leaves

Gordon's Bladderpod

Stems 4–14 inches; flowers have 4 petals; fruit a hollow sphere; oval to lance-shaped leaves

Yellow Stonecrop

Spreading, mat-forming stems; flowers have 5 pointed petals; tubular, succulent leaves

Solidago altissima

Tall Goldenrod

Stems 2–6 feet; flowers in plumelike clusters, tiny rays; scratchy, lance-shaped leaves

Thymophylla pentachaeta

Fiveneedle Dogweed

Stems 4–8 inches; long flower stalks, dime-sized flower head; leaves have stiff, threadlike lobes

Tribulus terrestris

Goathead

Mat-forming stems to 3 feet wide; 5 yellow petals; fruit a thorny nutlet; elliptic leaflets

Oxalis dillenii

Yellow Wood Sorrel

Stems 4–10 inches; 5 solid-yellow petals with notched tips; leaves have 3 heart-shaped leaflets

Asclepias tuberosa

Butterfly Milkweed

Hairy stems to 3 feet; yellow to orange flowers; hairy, narrow, lance-shaped leaves; clear sap

Berberis trifoliolata

Agarita

Shrub 3–6 feet; clustered fragrant flowers, 6 small petals; red berry; 3 gray-green, spiny leaflets

Cevallia sinuata

Stinging Cevallia

Stems 1–3 feet, foliage with stinging hairs; flowers in a dense cluster; lance-shaped, lobed leaves

Chamaesaracha conioides

False Nightshade

Stems 4–12 inches; petals creamy, united with a central star pattern; hairy leaves with wrinkled lobes

Yellow to Orange

Damianita
Rounded and shrubby, 1–2 feet tall; flower stems well above foliage; needlelike, crowded leaves

Scrambled Eggs
Stems 8–18 inches; spike of flowers, petals form curved tube with spur; leaflets parsleylike

Christmas Cactus
Stem jointed, thorny, bushy to 5 feet; pale yellow flower; red, fleshy, cylindrical fruit

Giant Helleborine Orchid
Leafy stems 1–3 feet; orangish-brown flowers with reddish streaks; clasping leaves; streamsides

Bitterweed
Stems 1–2 feet; yellow ray flowers with toothed tips; disk yellow or brown; threadlike leaves

Gray Golden Aster
Stems 8–16 inches; yellow ray flowers and disk; densely hairy, lance-shaped leaves

Camphor Weed
Stems 1–5 feet; yellow ray flowers and disk; rough, camphor-scented, lance-shaped leaves

Hog Potato
Stems 6–12 inches; stem and flower dotted with red glands; oval leaflets along midrib

Hypoxis hirsuta

Yellow Star Grass

Leafless flower stems 2–7 inches; star-shaped flowers with 6 petals; grasslike leaves from bulb

Kallstroemia parviflora

Warty Caltrop

Mat-forming stems 20–40 inches long; 5 orange petals with reddish tint; elliptical leaflets

Larrea tridentata

Creosote Bush

Rounded desert shrub; 5 twisted, propellerlike petals; fuzzy white fruit; aromatic leaves

Ludwigia octovalvis

Narrow-leaf Water Primrose

Bushy stems to 3 feet; 4 lemon-yellow petals; narrow, lance-shaped leaves; wetlands

Monarda punctata

Spotted Beebalm

Whorled clusters; tubular yellow (white or purple) spotted flowers with showy pink bracts

Oenothera laciniata

Cutleaf Evening Primrose

Sprawling hairy stems to 18 inches; flower has 4 heart-shaped petals; deeply lobed leaves

Physalis cinerascens

Smallflower Groundcherry

Sprawling stems to 18 inches; nodding bell-shaped flowers with a dark base; hairy, oval leaves

Senna roemeriana

Two-leaf Senna

Stems 1–2 feet; flowers have 5 wrinkled petals, showy brown stamens; paired leaflets

Tetraneuris scaposa

Four-nerve Daisy (Bitterweed)
Stems 6–16 inches; rays have 3 notches, 4 lengthwise veins; narrow to oval basal leaves

Thelesperma megapotamicum

Navajo Tea
Flower stalks 12–32 inches tall; disk has flowers only, no rays; leaves have threadlike lobes

Verbascum thapsus

Woolly Mullein
Bloom stalks to 6 feet; spikes of yellow flowers, 5 petals; large, fuzzy leaves; roadside invasive

Sonchus asper

Sow-Thistle
Stems 1–6 feet; ray flowers only, tips with tiny teeth; prickly, clasping leaves; milky sap

Packera tampicana

Butterweed
Stems 8–20 inches; 8–18 rays around yellow disk; narrow leaflets tipped with toothy lobes

Senecio ampullaceus

Texas Groundsel
Stems 1–2 feet; clusters of yellow flowers; 8 rays, yellow disk; clasping oval to lance-shaped leaves

Senecio flaccidus

Threadleaf Groundsel
Stems 1–4 feet; clusters of flower; 8 or 13 narrow rays; gray-woolly, threadlike leaflets

Coreopsis tinctoria

Golden Tickseed
Stems 1–4 feet; 8 yellow rays with maroon basal spot; red-brown disk; threadlike leaflets

Chamaecrista fasciculata

Partridge Pea
Stems 1–3 feet; petals with red spot, showy brown stamens; flat, linear pods; paired, linear leaflets

Baptisia bracteata

Plains Wild Indigo
Stems 8–16 inches; dangling cascades of creamy-yellow flowers; 3 oval, pointed leaflets

Grindelia squarrosa

Curlycup Gumweed
Stems 1–3 feet; flower heads resinous, sticky; rays usually absent; lance-shaped, toothed leaves

Lindheimera texana

Texas Star
Stems 4–24 inches; flower head star-shaped, tips of rays notched; oval to lance-shaped leaves

Linum berlandieri

Berlandier's Flax
Stems 6–18 inches: petals yellow-orange with radiating red lines; narrow, linear, clasping leaves

Lithospermum incisum

Fringed Puccoon
Stems 6–12 inches; trumpet-shaped flowers, crinkly-edged lobes; linear to oblong leaves

Ranunculus macranthus

Large Buttercup
Stems 1–3 feet; flowers packed with petals and stamens; leaves have 3–5 hairy, lobed leaflets

Solanum rostratum

Buffalo Bur
Spiny stems 1–3 feet; flowers have 5 tissuelike petals, showy stamens; spiny lobed leaves

Sphaeralcea coccinea

Caliche Globemallow

Bushy, 1–2 feet tall; cup-shaped, salmon-orange flowers; leaves have 3–5 deep, fingerlike lobes

Sphaeralcea hastulata

Spear Globemallow

Stems 6–12 inches; orange-red flowers; hairy, lance-shaped leaves with 2 pointed basal lobes

Taraxacum officinale

Dandelion

Hollow stems 1–10 inches; flower head has 100+ rays, no disk; arrow-shaped leaf lobes

Thelesperma filifolium

Greenthread

Stems 4–24 inches; 8 rays have lobed tips, yellow or brown disk; threadlike leaves

Viguiera dentata

Plateau Golden-Eye

Stems 3–6 feet; 10–14 rays with notched tip; yellow disk; oval to lance-shaped, serrated leaves

Viguiera stenoloba

Skeleton-leaf Goldeneye

Bushy, 2–5 feet; long-stemmed flower heads; rays veined, yellow disk; threadlike leaves

Wedelia acapulcensis

Hairy Wedelia

Stems 1–3 feet; long-stemmed flowers; rays with 1 notch; lance-shaped, rough, hairy leaves

Xanthisma spinulosum

Spiny Golden Aster

Stems 6–18 inches; flower heads with 14–60 narrow rays; yellow disk; bristly leaf lobes

Yellow to Orange

Xanthisma texanum

Texas Sleepy Daisy
Stems 1–3 feet; 12–34 sharp-pointed ray flowers; linear to lance-shaped, hairless leaves

Zinnia grandiflora

Plains Zinnia
Clumps to 8 inches tall; 3–6 oval, bright-yellow rays, orange disk; thin, linear leaves

Amblyolepis setigera

Huisache Daisy
Stems 6–15 inches; rays with notched tips; yellow disk; oval to lance-shaped, smooth leaves

Baileya multiradiata

Desert Marigold
Stems 12–18 inches; head packed with rays with 3 notches; yellow disk; woolly, lobed leaves

Berlandiera lyrata

Chocolate Flower
Stems 1–2 feet; rays have notched tips, red veins underneath; maroon disk; lobed leaves

Coryphantha missouriensis

Nipple Cactus
Round stem 2–4 inches high; yellowish-green, narrow, pointed petals; oval, red fruit

Engelmannia peristenia

Cutleaf Daisy
Stems 1–2 feet tall; 8–10, oval, notched rays; yellow disk; leaves deeply lobed along midrib

Psilostrophe tagetina

Woolly Paper Flower
Stems 4–20 inches; 3–4 oval, notched rays; disk flowers protrude; woolly, oval leaves

Oenothera berlandieri

Square-bud Sundrops

Stems 6–24 inches; petals crinkly, disklike stigma black or yellow; keeled buds; narrow leaves

Pyrrhopappus pauciflorus

Texas Dandelion

Stems 6–18 inches; rays have toothed tips; disk has dark anthers; lobed, toothed leaves

Helianthus petiolaris

Plains Sunflower

Stems 1–3 feet; showy rays; disk brown, center often whitish; triangular to lance-shaped leaves

Helianthus annuus

Annual Sunflower

Single stems 2–8 feet, 20+ flowers; rays yellow, disk reddish-brown; triangular leaves

Helianthus maximiliani

Maximilian Sunflower

Multiple stems 3–10 feet; flowers in leaf axils; rays, disk yellow; lance-shaped leaves, wavy edges

Cucurbita foetidissima

Buffalo Gourd

Sprawling stems; flowers with 5 large petals; fruit a green-striped ball; scratchy, ill-smelling leaves

Echinocereus dasyacanthus

Texas Rainbow

Cylindrical stems 4–9 inches tall; yellow petals with greenish base; barrel-shaped purple fruit

Oenothera macrocarpa

Fluttermill

Stems 4–18 inches; rounded petals; seed capsule with 4 wings; leathery, lance-shaped leaves

Verbesina encelioides

Cowpen Daisy

Stems 1–3 feet; rays with 3 deep notches; yellow disk; broad, toothed, rough, triangular leaves

Opuntia engelmannii

Englemann's Prickly Pear

Shrubby to 4 feet high with oval pads; petals uniformly yellow; barrel-shaped purple fruit

Opuntia macrorhiza

Grassland Prickly Pear

Sprawling clumps, 1–2 pads high; pads wrinkled, 3–5 inches; yellow petals, red base; red fruit

Opuntia phaeacantha

Brown-spine Prickly Pear

Clumps 1–2 feet high; oval pads, 4–13 inches long; yellow petals, red base; red fruit

Opuntia polyacantha

Plains Prickly Pear

Clumps sprawling, 1–2 pads high; wrinkled pads, 3–5 inches; yellow petals; tan, dry fruit

Ratibida columnifera

Prairie Coneflower

Stems 1–4 feet; yellow, maroon, or blended rays; brown cylindrical disk; lobed leaves

Rudbeckia hirta

Black-eyed Susan

Stems 1–3 feet; rays may have red base; domed, brown disk; hairy, lance-shaped to oval leaves

Silphium asteriscus

Starry Rosinweed

Stems 2–6 feet; notched rays; yellow disk; unlobed, lance-shaped, rough-hairy leaves

Red to Pink

Sand Verbena
Sprawling-erect stems 12–18 inches; 3-inch spherical clusters of tubular flowers; sticky oval leaves

Shaggy Portulaca
Sprawling stems have tufts of hair around flowers with 5 oval petals; tubular, succulent leaves

Catclaw Mimosa
Thorny shrub to 6 feet; fragrant, filamentlike flowers in spherical clusters; 5–12 pairs of leaflets

Trailing Windmills
Stems prostrate 1–3 feet; 3 fan-shaped rose to magenta petals; oblong, sticky leaves

Indian (Texas) Paintbrush
Flowers creamy tubes surrounded by red, rounded, unlobed bracts; hairy narrow, linear leaves

Prairie Paintbrush
Flowers greenish tubes surrounded by red, pink, yellow, or whitish bracts; leaves with narrow lobes

Mountain Pink
Stems rounded 4–12 inch tall clusters; 5 star-shaped pink petals; narrow, linear leaves

Ocotillo
Stems wandlike, thorny, 8–20 feet; tubular flowers in spike on tips; leaves found only after rains

Red to Pink

Scarlet Pea
Sprawling stems form mats to 4-feet wide; pealike flowers; leaves have 5–9 leaflets

Trailing Krameria
Stems sprawling, hairy 8–40 inches; flowers have 4–5 wine-red sepals; linear, pointed leaves

Henbit
Stems 2–14 inches; tubular, pink to purple flowers in whorls; round-ed leaves; weedy; introduced

California Loosestrife
Branching stems to 2 feet; tubular, rose-purple flowers, white throat; linear to lance-shaped leaves

Sensitive Briar
Spreading prickly stems; flowers in spherical clusters with showy filaments; leaflets fold if touched

Meadow Four-O'Clock
Stems 1–3 feet tall; pink, magenta, or white flowers; linear, lance-shaped, or oval leaves

Lemon Beebalm
Stems 1–2 feet; pinkish flowers in dense whorls, pale to rose-purple bracts; lance-shaped leaves

Velvet-leaf Gaura
Stems 2–7 feet; arching spikes have tiny pink to white flowers; oval leaves, covered with soft hairs

Scarlet Gaura

Stems hairy, 8–20 inches; flowers open white at night, turn red next day; erect, cylindrical buds

Small Palafoxia

Stems 7–24 inches; curly, pink pompom-like florets; hairy, narrow, linear leaves

Meadow Pink

Stems 6–20 inches; star-shaped flowers with a yellow eye; clasping oval to lance-shaped leaves

Scarlet Tropical Sage

Stems 1–3 feet; flowers in whorls on spike; heart-shaped, veined leaves; eastern half of Texas

Cedar Sage

Stems 1–2 feet; flowers in whorls on spike; heart-shaped, veined leaves; western half of Texas

Texas Thistle

Stems 2–5 feet; flower head has ¼-inch spines; oblong leaves, lobes with ¼-inch spines

Yellow-spine Thistle

Stems 1–3 feet; flower head has ½-inch spines; leaf lobes twisted, spines ¾-inch long

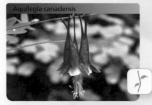

Red Columbine

Up to 3 feet tall; nodding flowers have yellowish-tipped petals and long, straight, red spurs

Scarlet Leatherflower

Vines to 9 feet long; 1-inch-long leathery urn-shaped flowers; endemic to central Texas

Standing Cypress

Stems 2–6 feet; tubular flowers, 5-pointed lobes, orange dots inside; narrow, linear leaflets

Turk's Cap

Plants 2–5 feet; petals fold around erect stamens; velvety, heart-shaped leaves

Scarlet Musk-Flower

Stems 4–16 inches; rounded clusters of musky-smelling flowers; hairy, triangular leaves

Rose Pavonia

Shrubby, 1–3 feet tall; flowers have 5 rounded petals, extended stamens; velvety, oval leaves

Cutleaf Penstemon

Stems 1–3-feet; flowers tubular with white throat; oval leaves lined with small teeth

Meadow Beauty

Stems to 2-feet; flowers have pink to whitish petals, showy yellow anthers; elliptic leaves

Cardinal Catchfly

Stems 1–2 feet; tubular flowers with deeply cut, pointed petals; sticky linear to elliptic leaves

Winecup

Stems 6–12 inches; flowers reddish purple, white centers; leaves with 5–7 hairy lobes

Beehive Cactus

Stems cylindrical to 8 inches tall; flowers at stem apex with many slender, pointed petals

Cardinal Flower

Stems 2–6 feet tall; trumpet-shaped flowers with 5 spreading lobes; oblong to lance-shaped leaves

Coral Honeysuckle

Woody vine to 15 feet long; whorled clusters of tubular flowers with 5 lobes; elliptical leaves

Texas Skeleton Plant

Stems 10–25 inches; 8–12 pink to lavender petals tipped with teeth; scalelike leaves; milky sap

Scarlet Penstemon

Stems hairy, 18–25 inches; flower lobes have dark lines, a white throat; lance-shaped leaves

Obedient Plant

Stems 1–3 feet; cylindrical spike of pink to lavender, tubular flowers; toothed, lance-shaped leaves

Red Prickly Poppy

Prickly stems to 3 feet, yellow sap; petals burgundy to white, tissue-papery; spine-tipped leaf lobes

Trumpet Creeper Vine

Woody vine climbing to 35 feet; red-orange, trumpet-shaped flowers; paired, toothed oval leaflets

Musk Thistle

Spiny stems to 15 feet; flower heads nod, spiny base, pink-purple florets; spiny leaves; invasive

Bull Thistle

Stems 1–6 feet tall; flower heads with red, purple, or yellow florets; leaves have purple spines

Purple Coneflower

Stems 1–4 feet; pink to purple rays droop slightly; reddish-yellow disk; lance-shaped leaves

Cane Cholla Cactus

Cylindrical stems 3–9 feet tall have wicked spines and barbed bristles; pink to magenta flowers

Devil's Head Cactus

Barrel cactus to 16 inches tall; flowers pink to magenta at woolly apex; straight to curved spines

Horse Crippler Cactus

Rounded, ribbed stem to 8 inches tall; flowers circle apex; pink to orange petals, edges fringed

Claret Cup Cactus

Ribbed, cylindrical, clumping stems to 4 inches wide; firm, spoon-shaped, waxy-looking petals

Strawberry Cactus

Ribbed, cylindrical, clumping stems to 4 inches wide; tissuelike, petals, tips flexible; oval red fruit

Strawberry Hedgehog

Ribbed, cylindrical, clumping stems; dense straw-colored spines; petals red to magenta

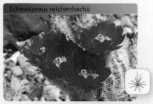

Lace Cactus

Cylindrical stems covered with lacy spines; rose-pink to magenta petals

Indian Blanket

Stems to 2 feet; rays with varying amounts of yellow and red; linear to spatula-shaped leaves

Sharp-pod Morning Glory

Twining vine; pink to lavender flowers with purple throat; heart-shaped leaves with 3–5 lobes

Pink Evening Primrose

Stems to 20 inches; flowers rosy-pink to whitish, nodding buds; lance-shaped to elliptic leaves

Prairie Rose

Climbing stems 6–15 feet high with prickles; flowers pink to white; 3–5 elliptical to lance-shaped leaflets

Basket Flower

Stems 2–5 feet; center florets white, outer ones pink; oval to lance-shaped leaves

White to Green

Abronia fragrans

Fragrant Sand-verbena
Sticky, hairy stems 10–40 inches; spherical clusters of fragrant, flowers; lance-shaped leaves

Achillea millefolium

Common Yarrow
Stems 1–3 feet tall; flat clusters of tiny white flowers; aromatic fernlike leaves

Bifora americana

Prairie Bishop's Weed
Stems 10–30 inches; spoked arrays tipped with clusters of small flowers; threadlike leaves

Cephalanthus occidentalis

Buttonbush
Shrubby 3–15 feet; spherical clusters; tiny flowers, protruding stamens; elliptic leaves; streamsides

Cicuta maculata

Spotted Water Hemlock
Stems 2–9 feet, purple spotted; arrays tipped with clusters of small flowers; lance-shaped leaflets

Dalea candida

White Prairie-Clover
Clumping stems 2 feet tall; dense spikes; tiny flowers, yellow anthers; leaflets oblong to linear

Daucus pusillus

Wild Carrot
Stems 1–3 feet; spoked array tipped with clusters of small flowers; parsleylike leaflets

Eriogonum annuum

Annual Buckwheat
Hairy stems 1–3 feet; small flowers in dense clusters; white petals, red sepals; oblong leaves

White to Green

Euphorbia bicolor

Snow-on-the-Prairie
Stems 1–5 feet; tiny flowers; long, narrow, bicolored bracts; lance-shaped, hairy leaves; milky sap

Euphorbia marginata

Snow-on-the-Mountain
Stems 1–3 feet; tiny, white flowers; oval bicolored bracts; smooth oval leaves; milky sap

Hymenopappus scabiosaeus

Old Plainsman
Stem 2–5 feet; flower head has tiny, petal-like bracts around white disk; narrow, lobed leaflets

Lepidium virginicum

Pepper Grass
Clumps 6–24 inches tall; cylindrical spike; 4 petals on flowers; flat, round seeds; linear upper leaves

Polygala alba

Milkwort
Stems 6–16 inches; spike of flowers with 3 united petals, 2 side wings; narrow, linear leaves

Plantago patagonica

Woolly Plantain
Bloom stems 4–10 inches; cylindric, woolly spike, petals greenish-white; long, narrow leaves

Rivina humilis

Pigeonberry
Sprawling shrub 1–6 feet; spike of small white to pink flowers; red berries; triangular leaves

Saururus cernuus

Lizard's Tail
Wetland colonies with 3-foot stems; tiny white flowers in drooping spike; heart-shaped leaves

White to Green

Toxicoscordion nuttallii

Death Camas

Stems 12–30 inches; dense cluster; petals with yellowish basal spot; grasslike leaves from bulb

Trifolium repens

White Clover

Stems 4–10 inches; spherical clusters, pealike flowers; leaves with 3 rounded leaflets

Verbesina virginica

Frostweed

Winged stems 3–6 feet; dense flower clusters; small, white rays; white disk; lance-shaped leaves

Eysenhardtia texana

Texas Kidneywood

Branching shrub 4–10 feet; fragrant flowers on showy spikes; leaves have many oval leaflets

Aphanostephus ramosissimus

Plains Doze Daisy

Stems 4–20 inches; rays have red stripe below; yellow disk; linear to lobed leaves

Chaetopappa ericoides

Baby Aster

Stems 2–7 inches; rays fade to pink, tips curl; narrow leaves overlapping against stem

Symphyotrichum ericoides

White Aster

Stems 1–3 feet; tight clusters of flower heads; narrow rays; yellow disk; crowded, linear leaves

Erigeron modestus

Plains Fleabane

Stems 3–12 inches; white rays, red-tinted backs; yellow disk, pink buds; spoon-shaped leaves

White to Green

Erigeron philadelphicus

Philadelphia Fleabane
Stems 8–30 inches; flower heads with 150+ rays; leaves oblong to lance-shaped, clasping

Spiranthes cernua

Nodding Lady's Tresses
Stems 6–16 inches; spiraling spike of tubular flowers, slightly nodding; leaves oval to elliptic

Allium drummondii

Drummond Wild Onion
Stems 4–12 inches: umbrellalike flower cluster; white to pink, red-striped petals; aromatic leaves

Nothoscordum bivalve

Crow Poison
Stems 6–20 inches; umbrellalike flower cluster; yellow anthers; grasslike, odorless leaves

Asclepias asperula

Antelope Horns Milkweed
Clumps 1–3 feet; spherical flower clusters; conical pods, fluffy seeds; narrow leaves; milky sap

Asclepias oenotheroides

Zizotes Milkweed
Stems 1–2 feet; loose clusters in leaf axils; conical pods, fluffy seeds; oval leaves; milky sap

Dimorphocarpa candicans

Palmer's Spectacle Pod
Stem 16–30 inches: petals white to lavender; seed disks paired; woolly, folded leaves

Delphinium carolinianum ssp. virescens

Carolina Larkspur
Stems 1–3 feet; flowers white to blue; rear spur points upward; roundish, lobed leaves

White to Green

Desmanthus illinoensis

Illinois Bundleweed
Stems 2–3 feet; spherical clusters of tiny, tubular flowers; pods in tight bundle; fernlike leaves

Clematis drummondii

Old Man's Beard
Sprawling vine; creamy flowers, no petals; seeds a mass of feathery plumes; lobed leaflets

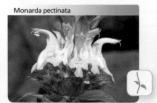
Monarda pectinata

Plains Beebalm
Hairy stems to 20 inches; whorled clusters with green bracts; oblong to lance-shaped leaves

Polanisia dodecandra

Clammyweed
Stems 8–24 inches; dense cluster; white petals, long purple stamens; sticky, fetid leaflets

Zinnia acerosa

Dwarf Zinnia
Clumps 4–18 inches tall; oblong rays; yellow disk turning brown; narrow, crowded leaves

Convolvulus equitans

Texas Bindweed
Twining stems to 6 feet long; white to pink flower; narrow leaves with rear lobes

Mammillaria heyderi

Nipple Cactus
Stems flat-topped, 3–6 inches wide; flowers circle top; red fruit lasts all winter; straight spines

Melampodium leucanthum

Blackfoot Daisy
Stems 6–16 inches; narrow, notched rays; yellow disk; hairy, linear to lance-shaped leaves

White to Green

Rubus trivialis

Dewberry
Prickly low vine; 5 crinkly petals; red fruit turning black; 3–5 pointed, toothed leaflets

Penstemon laxiflorus

Loose-flowered Penstemon
Stems 1–2 feet; nodding flowers, beard tongue golden; toothed, clasping, lance-shaped leaves

Penstemon cobaea

Foxglove
Stems 1–2 feet; flowers a white to pinkish inflated tube, beard tongue golden, streaked throat

Pinaropappus roseus

White Dandelion
Stems 6–12 inches; rays have yellow bases, pink-striped below, tips toothed; narrow leaves

Yucca constricta

Buckley Yucca
Flower stalk 3–6 feet above leaves; bell-shaped flowers; swordlike, spine-tipped leaves

Yucca rupicola

Twisted-leaf Yucca
Flower stalk 2–5 feet above leaves; bell-shaped flowers; flexible, spine-tipped leaves

Yucca treculeana

Trecul Yucca
Trunk to 10 feet; branching cluster within leaves; swordlike, spine-tipped leaves

Zephyranthes chlorosolen

Rain Lily
Flower stem 6–12 inches; floral tube 3–4 inches with 6 pointed lobes; grasslike leaves

White to Green

Argemone albiflora

White Prickly Poppy
Prickly stems 2–4 feet; flowers have 6 crinkly petals; yellow filaments; lobed, prickly leaves

Datura wrightii

Sacred Datura
Sprawling stems 3–4 feet; trumpet-shaped flowers; spiny fruit; oval to triangular leaves

Hibiscus laevis

Halberd-leaf Rosemallow
Stems 3–6 feet; petals whitish with a purple base; triangular leaves with pointed basal lobes

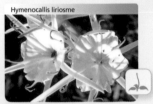
Hymenocallis liriosme

Spring Spider Lily
Stems 1–3 feet; cuplike flowers have long, slender segments; leaves are long, flat blades

Mentzelia nuda

Bractless Blazingstar
Stems 3–5 feet; long narrow petals; toothed, lance-shaped leaves covered with barbed hairs

Oenothera albicaulis

Prairie Evening Primrose
Sprawling stems 1–2 feet; 4 heart-shaped petals, buds nod; wavy to lobed, hairy leaves

Proboscidea louisianica

Devil's Claw
Sprawling stem 1–3 feet; white to pale lavender trumpet-shaped flowers; fruit a hooked pod

Silphium albiflorum

White Rosinweed
Stems 8–36 inches; white notched rays; white disk florets; deeply lobed, sandpapery leaves

Blue to Purple

Nuttall's Milkvetch
Stems to 18 inches; lilac and white pealike flowers; flat, curved pods; leaves have 7–23 leaflets

Mist Flower
Stems to 3 feet; clusters of tiny, fluffy, blue-purple flowers; oval to triangular veined, toothed leaves

Purple Prairie Clover
Stems leafy, 15–30 inches; cylindrical spikes of purple flowers; 5-7 narrow, linear leaflets

Feather Dalea
Low-mounding shrub 2–3 feet; violet flowers with a yellow lobe, hairy plumes; tiny, oblong leaflets

Dakota Vervain
Sprawling stems 4–24 inches; rounded clusters of purple to pink flowers; lobed leaves

Purplemat
Low mounds 4–20 inches wide; lavender to purple, throat yellow; hairy leaves, edges rolled under

Baby Blue Eyes
Stems to 12 inches; flowers blue-lavender, solitary on stems; leaves have oval, pointed lobes

Blue Phacelia
Stems to 12 inches; blue-lavender flowers in tight clusters; leaves have shallow lobes

Phacelia congesta

Blue Curls
Stems to 3 feet; bell-shaped, blue to purple flowers in a coiled cluster; leaves with rounded lobes

Scutellaria drummondii

Skullcap
Hairy stems 8–12 inches tall; lobed lower lip has white bars, purple spots; hairy, oval leaves

Verbena halei

Texas Vervain
Stems 12–18 inches; flowers blue to lavender, ¼-inch-wide; narrow, linear to lobed leaves

Vernonia baldwinii

Western Ironweed
Clumps 2–5 feet tall; threadlike flower heads; finely toothed, elliptic to lance-shaped leaves

Vicia ludoviciana

Deer Pea Vetch
Sprawling to 3 feet; spikes of pealike flowers; leaves have paired leaflets and tendril at tip

Anemone berlandieri

Wind Flower
Stem 6–18 inches with 3 whorled, leaflike bracts; lavender to white flowers; lobed leaflets

Camassia scilloides

Wild Hyacinth
Stem with flower spike to 30 inches tall; lilac to pale blue petals; long, linear leaves from bulb

Clematis pitcheri

Purple Leatherflower
Low-climbing vine; nodding, urn-shaped flowers, leathery petals; leaves have 3 oval leaflets

Blue to Purple

Ground Plum

Sprawling stems; purple, pinkish to whitish flowers; spherical fleshy pod; elliptic leaflets

Buffalo Clover

Stems sprawling; flowers blue to purple, center white with lines; flat, curved pod; leaf top hairless

Missouri Milkvetch

Sprawling stems; purple-pinkish flowers, white center; hairy straight pods; hairy leaflets

Blue Prairie Larkspur

Stems 1–3 feet; blue to whitish flowers; rear spur points upward; leaves roundish, lobed

Stork's Bill

Sprawling stems; lavender-purple flowers, yellow stamens; long, conical seeds; round lobed leaves

Eryngo

Stems to 3 feet; flower head purple with spiny, purple bracts; spiny-lobed, purple leaves

Big Bend Bluebonnet

Stems 3–4 feet; long spike of purple-blue flowers with white patch; elliptic leaflets; found in west Texas

Texas Bluebonnet

Stems 6–24 inches; spike tipped with white buds; flowers with white patch; elliptic leaflets

Blue to Purple

Liatris punctata

Gay Feather
Stems 1–3 feet; plumelike spikes with dense lavender florets; narrow, linear leaves

Maurandella antirrhiniflora

Snapdragon Vine
Low-climbing vine; small tubular flowers with spreading lobes, white throat; triangular leaves

Nuttallanthus texanus

Texas Toadflax
Stems to 30 inches; flowers light-blue to whitish, down-curved rear spur; linear to oval leaves

Oxalis drummondii

Drummond's Wood Sorrel
Flower stems to 12 inches; petals lined purplish to pink; 3 deeply lobed, winglike leaflets

Oxytropis lambertii

Purple Locoweed
Plant silky-hairy; flower stems to 12 inches; cylindrical pods; leaves have 7–19 linear leaflets

Penstemon fendleri

Fendler Penstemon
Stems 12–18 inches; flowers in whorled clusters, violet-lavender, lined throat; elliptic leaves

Phlox drummondii

Drummond's Phlox
Stems 6–18 inches; lavender, pink, red flowers; center white or a red star; lance-shaped leaves

Giliastrum acerosum

Bluebowls, Blue Gilia
Densely branched to 6 inches; bright blue flowers with yellow anthers; needlelike leaves

Blue to Purple

Purple Groundcherry
Mat-forming stems 4–6 inches high; crinkly petals, yellow anthers; berry in lanternlike sack

Shrubby Blue Sage
Bushy 2–6 feet; hairy upper petal, lobed lower petal; veiny, triangular to oblong leaves

Engelmann's Sage
Stems 6–15 inches; light-blue, white-spotted flowers in dense spike; narrow, hairy leaves

Mealy Blue Sage
Stems woolly, 1–3 feet; white-spotted lower petal; lance-shaped, toothed leaves

Lyre-leaf Sage
Stems 1–2 feet; narrowly tubular flowers in separated whorls; deeply lobed basal leaves

Texas Sage
Hairy, stems 6–18 inches; flowers white-spotted in few-flowered clusters; lance-shaped leaves

Blue-eyed Grass
Clumps 6–18 inches; light-blue to violet lined petals, yellow center; grasslike leaves

Texas Mountain Laurel
Tree to 15 feet; dangling clusters of purple flowers, scented like grape Kool-Aid; oval leaflets

Triodanis perfoliata

Venus's Looking Glass
Stems 4–36 inches; flowers have white throat; roundish leaves clasp stem; milky sap

Viola missouriensis

Missouri Violet
Stems 2–4 inches; violet pale-blue to whitish flowers; purple veins; heart-shaped leaf bases

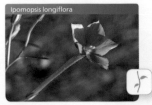
Ipomopsis longiflora

Pale Trumpets
Stems 4–24 inches; long, tubular, blue to whitish flowers; narrow, linear leaves

Linum lewisii

Blue Flax
Stems 1–2 feet; lined light to dark blue flowers, yellow center; narrow leaves hug stem

Machaeranthera tanacetifolia

Tansy Daisy
Clumping stems to 1 foot; purple to violet flower rays, yellow disk; fernlike, spine-tipped leaves

Symphyotrichum pratense

Meadow Aster
Stems 15–24 inches; 15–25 purple ray flowers; yellow to whitish disk; firm, elliptical leaves

Solanum dimidiatum

Western Horse Nettle
Prickly stems 1–3 feet; wrinkled purple to violet petals; toxic yellow berries; lobed, scratchy leaves

Solanum elaeagnifolium

Silver-leaf Nightshade
Prickly stems 1–3 feet; wrinkled petals; toxic yellow berries; narrow to oblong silvery-hairy leaves

Blue to Purple

Commelina erecta

Widow's Tears
Fleshy stems 6–18 inches; 2 rounded blue petals, 1 small white petal; bladelike leaves

Tradescantia occidentalis

Western Spiderwort
Fleshy stems to 20 inches; 3 blue to rose oval petals; narrow, bladelike leaves sheathing stem

Nemastylis geminiflora

Celestials
Stems 5–12 inches; dark to light blue flowers, white center; long, narrow leaves with pleated folds

Ruellia nudiflora

Wild Petunia
Stems 1–2 feet; trumpet-shaped flowers, blue to purple petals, crinkly; toothed, elliptical leaves

Alophia drummondii

Propeller Flower
Stems 1–2 feet; irislike flower, yellow center with reddish marks; leaves are long, pleated blades

Eustoma exaltatum

Texas Bluebell
Stems 2–3 feet; bell-shaped blue to lavender flowers, center dark purple; elliptical, clasping leaves

Ipomoea lindheimeri

Lindheimer's Morning Glory
Low-climbing vine; trumpet-shaped light-blue flower; white throat; deeply lobed leaves

Passiflora incarnata

Purple Passionflower
Low-climbing vine; complex purple and white flower; hairlike filaments; lobed leaves

Adventure Quick Guides

Only Texas Wildflowers
Organized by color
for quick and easy identification

Simple and convenient—narrow your choices by color and leaf attachment, and view just a few wildflowers at a time

- Pocket-size format—easier than laminated foldouts

- Professional photos of flowers in bloom

- Similar colors grouped together to ensure that you quickly find what you're looking for

- Leaf icons for comparison and identification

- Easy-to-use information for even casual observers

- Expert author is a skilled botanist and photographer

Get these *Adventure Quick Guides* for your area

ISBN 978-1-59193-816-3   U.S. $9.95

5 0 9 9 5

PUBLICATIONS
Adventure
an imprint of Adventure**KEEN**

NATURE/WILDFLOWERS/TEXAS

9 781591 938163